Getting To Know...

Nature's Children

LOONS

Judy Ross

Facts in Brief

Classification of the Common Loon

    Class: *Aves* (birds)

    Order: *Gaviiformes* (loon-shaped birds)

    Family: *Gaviidae* (loon family)

    Genus: *Gavia*

    Species: *Gavia immer*

World distribution. Found with closely related species throughout the Northern Hemisphere.

Habitat. Northern wilderness lakes in summer; ocean coasts and southern lakes in winter.

Distinctive physical characteristics. Pointed bill; three-toed webbed feet set back toward its tail; in summer, white neck band, black back streaked with white; red eyes.

Habits. Almost wholly aquatic but nests at water's edge; lives alone or in pairs; migrates southward for the winter; foot-propelled deep diver.

Diet. Small fish, insects, frogs, weeds, crustaceans.

Canadian Cataloguing in Publication Data

Ross, Judy, 1942-
  Loons

(Getting to know—nature's children)
Includes index.
ISBN 0-7172-1915-1

1. Loons—Juvenile literature.
I. Title. II. Series.

QL696.G33R67 1985   j598.4'42   C85-098717-2

Have you ever wondered . . .

Have you ever heard someone say, "You're as crazy as a loon?" Some people think that expression got started because of the loon's ha-ha-ha call, which sounds a bit like mad laughter. Loons were once thought to be crazy because of this strange laughing call.

Today we know that there is nothing crazy about loons. But although they aren't crazy, they *are* remarkable in many ways. For instance, did you know that loons are such good underwater swimmers that they:
—could beat most fish in a race
—rarely set foot on land except to lay their eggs
—swim when they are only a few hours old
—can sink out of sight while swimming?

Curious? Let's find out more about this unusual water-loving bird with the unforgettable voice.

Water Babies

Loon chicks go for their first swim when they are only a few hours old, and in no time at all they are paddling contentedly around behind their parents. But loon babies are a bit like human babies; they get tired easily. Their mother will therefore take care not to swim too fast for them. And if they get too tired she will even let them scramble up onto her back and ride until they are rested and ready to swim again.

Because loons spend most of their lives in the water it is important for the chicks to become strong swimmers. Fortunately, swimming seems to come naturally to the loon chicks. Perhaps that is because they come from a family of superb swimmers and divers.

Young loons always stay close to their mother's side.

The Loon Family

There are four loon "cousins" in the family—the Yellow-billed, Red-throated, Arctic and Common loons. Each has its own special markings. Can you guess what is special about the Yellow-billed Loon? What about the Red-throated Loon? Their names will give you the answer. The Arctic Loon has a gray head and lives, as you might have guessed, in the Arctic.

To find out more about the fourth cousin— the Common Loon—turn the page.

It's easy to tell that this is a Red-throated Loon. Just look at the flash of color on its throat.

The Common Loon

Common Loons got their name because they are the loons we most often see. It is easy to tell the Common Loon from its cousins. In the spring and early summer, it has bright red eyes, a black-and-white checker-board coat and a thin "necklace" of white markings around its neck.

In late summer it sheds this coat. In its place the loon grows a drab gray winter outfit, and its white necklace almost disappears. Against this gray coat its eyes look more brown than red.

If you saw a male and female loon swimming together you would not be able to tell them apart. Unlike many birds, they both have the same markings.

A loon's bill is long, sharp and pointed—all the better to fish with.

Two Homes

The Common Loon has two homes. In summer it lives on northern and wilderness lakes in parts of North America, Iceland and Europe. But when its home lake freezes over in late fall, the loon must fly south. If it stays where it is, a covering of ice will cut the loon off from the fish it eats, and it will starve.

Some North American loons spend winters on the ocean where there is salt water which does not freeze. Others winter as far south as California and Florida.

A list of a loon's favorite food wouldn't be complete without the pickerel, bass and other fish—even frogs.

Built for Swimming

When you want to go for a swim, you put on a bathing suit and maybe even a bathing cap, swim fins and floats. A loon doesn't need any special equipment to go swimming. Its body is perfectly suited to live in the water.

The loon's body is torpedo-shaped so it can cut through the water smoothly and easily. To propel itself, the loon has big webbed feet set back toward its tail. Having its feet at the back of its body in this way gives the loon extra paddle power in the water. When the loon is swimming on the surface, it uses its feet like a miniature paddlewheel to push it forward. For underwater swimming the loon thrusts itself forward, using its feet like the propeller on a boat.

The loon's feathers are also ideal for life in the water. They grow so close together that no water can get through them. Besides waterproofing the loon, the feathers also trap air. This trapped air helps the loon float high in the water—even if several chicks are hitching a ride.

Opposite page:

Loons often rear up in the water, flap their wings, stretch their neck, shake their head, then settle back down.

Underwater Flyers

A loon is a superb diver and underwater swimmer. It dips, dives and soars underwater as if it were flying. It even "flaps" its wings underwater for a burst of extra speed or to help it change directions quickly.

To see a loon dive you must watch closely. If you blink you might miss it. The loon plunges forward with its neck arched and pushes itself down with its strong feet. It dives so quickly and quietly that it hardly leaves a ripple behind on the surface.

A good game is trying to figure out where the loon will resurface after a dive. It can swim great distances underwater, as far as a city block in less than a minute. Loons are deep divers too. A loon has been caught in a fisherman's net 70 metres (240 feet) below the surface!

Loon

Duck

Notice how much farther back the loon's legs are set than the duck's.

A mother loon may not dive when she senses danger. Instead she may dance on the water to draw attention away from her eggs.

The Loon on Land

The loon is a graceful and powerful swimmer, but on land it is so awkward that you might think it had two left feet. Because the loon's legs are toward the back of its body and its feet are large and webbed, it has trouble walking on land. Running is almost impossible. Sometimes a loon loses its balance altogether and flops over onto its stomach. Then it must flap its wings wildly to get up again. If it is tired, it might give up and push itself along the ground on its stomach.

The loon's clumsiness on land may be funny to watch, but it can be a problem for the loon. It cannot escape if a hungry mink or lynx or other loon enemy chases it on land. To avoid predators, loons only go on land when they are nesting. Even then, they build their nests at the edge of the water so that they can hop in and swim off if a predator comes near.

Being such clumsy walkers, loons wisely build their nests as near to water as possible.

Now You See It, Now You Don't

A swimming loon has a special trick that allows it to almost disappear when it is frightened. It can sink part way into the water so that less of its body can be seen. To do this, it squeezes its feathers together and gets rid of air trapped between them. And it forces the air out of its lungs. Without all that air to keep it afloat, it slowly sinks lower into the water.

Loons often try to keep out of sight by swimming close to reeds.

Fine Fisherman

Have you ever gone fishing? If you have you probably sat and sat waiting for a fish to nibble on your bait. What a pity you cannot fish the way a loon does. Instead of waiting for the fish to come to it, the loon jumps in the water and goes after the fish.

The loon dives for fish and traps them in its bill. A small fish is usually eaten underwater in one big gulp, but bigger fish are brought up to the surface before being swallowed whole. The loon mostly eats small fish and minnows.

Sometimes, when the loon is looking under water for its next meal, it munches on other underwater goodies such as frogs, weeds and even clams.

Nicknamed the "Great Northern Diver" the Common Loon can dive deeper than any other flying bird.

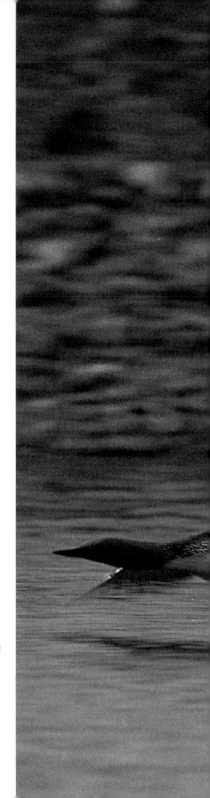

Take Off—Splash Down

Birds that spend a lot of time in the air cannot afford to carry around any extra weight. Their bones are filled with tiny pockets of air so that they weigh less. But the loon does not have these air-filled bones; it spends most of its life in or under water where heavier bones are useful.

What happens when the heavier-boned loon tries to take off? It really has to work at it. To get airborne, a loon needs a long water runway. It heads into the wind with its feet running madly on the water's surface. It half flies and half runs until it builds up enough speed to take off. Whew!

Once in the air, the loon looks hunchbacked. Its big webbed feet trail out behind its short tail, and its neck reaches downward as if it is looking at the water below all the time.

A loon landing is not a graceful sight. The loon zooms in low over the water, almost as if it cannot brake in the air, and belly flops down onto its breast. Then it skids through the water sending spray everywhere.

Loon Talk

Loons live alone or in pairs, rather than in large flocks. On a small lake you will usually find only one loon couple. On a larger lake there might be other pairs, but each pair will live in a separate bay. By spreading out in this way, the loons can be sure of finding enough food.

Even though loons rarely visit each other, they often "talk" to each other. When one loon cries out another will sometimes answer from a far away bay. This makes it sound as if the call is being echoed all across the lake .

The loon is well known for its distinctive calls. It has a mad, laughing ha-ha-ha call and a haunting wail that sounds like "Who-who-Who-Who-o-o-o." This lonely sounding call can often be heard at dusk or when a storm is approaching.

The haunting cry of a loon is so unusual that once you hear it you will never forget it.

Mating Dance

Loons are believed to choose a mate for life.
They do this by performing a mating dance
that looks like a beautiful water ballet.
Treading water side by side two courting loons
will suddenly take off and race wildly across
the water. At other times they swim slowly
toward each other.

When their bodies touch, they both stretch
their bills up into the air.

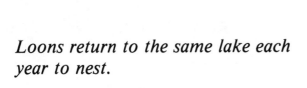

*Loons return to the same lake each
year to nest.*

A Water-side Nest

In early June, the loon pair choose a place for the female to lay the eggs. Often they will return to a place they have used before. If they cannot, they look for a rocky point of land or an island—always near water. Sometimes they will use a clump of floating weeds and plants as a ready-made nest, or even lay the eggs on the top of a muskrat house.

The mother loon lays two eggs that are about twice as big as chicken eggs. The loon eggs are greenish or brownish and speckled to blend in with the grasses and plants around the nest area. This camouflage helps hide the eggs from hungry egg-eaters such as otters, raccoons and skunks.

Mom and dad won't be long away from their two precious eggs.

Protective Parents

Sometimes the loon parents pull bits of weed and grass over the eggs to make them even more difficult for predators to find. Then the mother and father loon take turns sitting on the eggs to keep them safe and warm.

It takes about 30 days for the eggs to hatch, and parents must be constantly on the lookout for danger. If an enemy comes near the nest, the loon parents take to the water and swim away so that the location of the eggs is kept a secret. But there are other dangers besides predators. The eggs may be swept off their nest by the wash from a motorboat. Or they may be destroyed by the high waves of a bad storm.

Hatch Day

When the little chicks break out of their shells, they are wet and sticky and look as if they are all beaks and feet. The chick's soft down feathers are a dark brown-black. This coloring helps the chick blend in with the nest area so that it cannot be seen by hungry predators.

In just a few hours, the chicks are ready to leave the nest for good and begin their life in the water.

Whew! After all that hard work of cracking out of the egg, this loon chick is taking a rest.

Growing Up

The chicks learn to swim and dive by imitating their mother and father. The loon parents keep a close watch over their youngsters. They bring the chicks small fish to eat until the chicks can fish for themselves. Sometimes, instead of fish, the chicks eat a green salad made of water plants. When they have learned to swim and dive, the chicks start to fish for their own food.

Loon chicks eat a lot and grow quickly. By the end of summer their fluffy down molts, and they grow a new coat of gray feathers. These are flying feathers, and once they have grown in, the young loons begin to learn how to fly. By late September they are flying confidently and are almost fully grown.

This little loon must wait until it is at least 10 weeks old before it learns to fly.

The Flight South

The loons must leave their home lake when it ices over in late fall. They head south until they find a lake without ice, where they can still fish. When this lake freezes, they must fly still farther south in search of another open lake. Pushed farther and farther south by the weather, the loons hop from lake to lake. Finally they reach the ocean coasts or a southern lake where the water never freezes. Here they spend the winter, often in small groups.

Clumsy take-off!

On Their Own

The loons begin to fly north in the early spring. As soon as the ice breaks up on a lake or river, the loons are there. Hopping north lake by lake they return to their summer homes.

The young loons do not return to where they were hatched. Their parents are probably already there. Instead they look for a new lake or river where they will have enough food and a good choice of nesting sites.

Some loons arrive at the nesting ground with a mate. Others find a mate there. Once partners have been found, the young loons are ready to start families of their own.

Special Words

Camouflage Fur or feathers that blend in with an animal's surroundings so that it can avoid being seen.

Down A bird's first soft, fluffy feathers.

Mate To come together to produce young.

Markings Distinctive patterns or colors of fur or feathers.

Migrate To move from one place to another in search of food.

Molt To shed feathers before growing new ones.

Nesting site A place to build a nest.

Predator An animal that hunts other animals for food.

Webbed feet Feet in which the toes are joined together by flaps of skin.

INDEX

Cover Photo: Stephen Krasemann (Valan Photos)

Photo Credits: Wayne Lankinen (Valan Photos), pages 4, 40, 42; Pam Hickman (Valan Photos), pages 7, 34, 45; Stephen K. Krasemann (Valan Photos), pages 8, 24, 27; Ken Carmichael (Network Stock Photo File), pages 11, 37, 46; Brian Milne (First Light Associated Photographers), pages 13, 32; Brian Milne (Valan Photos), page 14; M.J. Johnson (Valan Photos), page 16; Esther Schmidt (Valan Photos), page 20; Barry Ranford, page 23; Michael McNall, page 29; Jacob Formsma (Network Stock Photo File), pages 30-31; James Richards, page 39.

Getting To Know...

Nature's Children

BLACK BEARS

Caroline Greenland

Grolier

Facts in Brief

Classification of the Black Bear

Class: *Mammalia* (mammals)
Order: *Carnivora* (meat-eaters)
Family: *Ursidae* (bear family)
Genus: *Ursus*
Species: *Ursus americanus*

World distribution. Exclusive to North America. Related species widely distributed throughout most of the Northern Hemisphere.

Habitat. Forest regions, swamps, and dense bushland.

Distinctive physical characteristics. Smallest of the North American bears; usually black with tan muzzle and white patch under throat; claws are comparatively short and curved.

Habits. Primarily solitary; fast runner; skilled tree climber; sleeps deeply for most of the winter; wanders far for food.

Diet. Plant life: roots, leaves, berries, grasses, fruit, and acorns; small mammals, frogs, fish, insects; honey.

Canadian Cataloguing in Publication Data

Greenland, Caroline.
  Black bears

(Getting to know—nature's children)
Includes index.
ISBN 0-7172-1911-9

1. Black bear—Juvenile literature.
I. Title. II. Series.

QL737.C27G73 1985   j599.74'446   C85-098705-9

Have you ever wondered . . .

Do you remember your very first Teddy Bear? It was probably soft and furry with little round ears, a black button nose and a squishy body just made for cuddling.

Children have had Teddies ever since the beginning of the century, when United States President Teddy Roosevelt saved a Black Bear cub from being killed. A toymaker, charmed by this story, decided that a bear would make a nice, huggable plaything for a child and created the first Teddy Bear.

Baby Black Bears look as huggable as toy Teddy Bears. But watch out! Their mother may be lurking nearby, ready to chase off anyone who comes near her babies.

These bears look cute and cuddly, but like all wild animals, they do not make good pets.

Bundles of Fun

Summertime is playtime for baby Black Bears. They chase butterflies, play tag and wrestle with each other, while their mother looks on.

If a hungry cougar or another bear comes too close, the mother shoos the cubs up the nearest tree. Then, growling fiercely, she scares off the intruder.

When the danger has passed, the mother calls to her babies, and they come shimmying down to the ground to play some more.

Once a cub is shooed up a tree by its mom, it may stay up for 20 hours or more until she says it's safe to come down again.

Black Bear

Brown Bear

Polar Bear

Bear Territory

Black Bears are the most common of the North American bears, and, compared to their relatives, the Brown and Polar Bears, they are also the smallest. Black Bears can be found across most of North America, up into Alaska and even as far south as Mexico. They prefer to live in thickly wooded areas or dense brushland, near a creek, stream or lake.

The Black Bears that live in North America have cousins in Asia. These Asiatic Black Bears are smaller than North American Black Bears and prefer to live in mountains and forests.

The Bear Facts

Male bears are also called boars. Black Bear boars weigh about 170 kilograms (375 pounds), which means it would take two fully grown men on one end of a teeter-totter to balance a Black Bear on the other end. Female bears, called sows, weigh slightly less than the males.

The shaded area shows where Black Bears are found.

Many-Colored Coat

Do not be fooled by their name. Not all Black Bears are black. Most are black with a brownish muzzle and a white throat patch or other white chest markings. But some Pacific Coast Black Bears are almost white; others are a bluish color. Cinnamon-colored Black Bears are quite common in Western Canada and the United States. In other areas, Black Bears may be brown, dark brown or even blue-black. Sometimes a mother will have cubs of different colors in the same litter, although this is unusual.

Whatever their color, all Black Bears have long, coarse fur that is not at all soft and cuddly like a Teddy Bear's coat. Every spring Black Bears shed their winter coat and grow a lighter-weight summer coat.

Scents, Sounds and Sights

The bear uses its long snout to sniff out other animals or a good supply of food, such as a patch of berries. To get a really big noseful of smells, a bear will often stand on its hind legs with its nose in the air.

A bear's rounded, furry ears are useful too. Its keen sense of hearing means it is difficult to sneak up on a bear without being noticed.

It is a good thing that a bear can smell and hear so well, because its eyesight is poor. In fact, a Black Bear has difficulty recognizing objects by sight. And Black Bears are color blind. This means they only see in shades of black, gray and white. They cannot see colors.

A Black Bear won't turn its nose up at very much. It will eat just about anything.

Bear Talk

If you overheard two Black Bears "talking," you would hear a strange combination of growls, whines and sniffs. Although you might have a problem understanding this "conversation," Black Bears do not. For instance, if a baby bear hears its mother making a sharp "woof-woof" sound, it knows danger is nearby. And every mother Black Bear knows that a baby-like cry means her young cub is in trouble—or hungry.

A bear often stands up to sniff the air for scents. It may even walk swaying its head from side to side, snuffling all the while.

Getting Around

Unlike many animals, but like you, bears put their whole foot, including their heel, on the ground when they walk. Because they do this with all four feet, they have an awkward, shambling walk. But if a bear is in a hurry, it can reach speeds of up to 55 kilometres (35 miles) per hour. A running bear looks a bit like a huge, black beachball bouncing through the woods.

Swimming is second nature to a Black Bear. It can "dog-paddle" across small lakes or rushing rivers with ease. When a Black Bear climbs out of the water it shakes itself dry like a big shaggy dog.

Black Bear paw prints

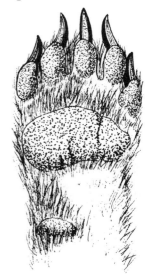

A bear usually travels along the same routes over and over again within its territory.

Front paw

Tree scratched by Black Bear

Opposite page:

The strong short claws of the Black Bear work much like grappling hooks when it is climbing a tree.

Going Up

If you were in a tree-climbing contest with a Black Bear, the bear would probably win. A Black Bear climbs trees to escape danger or to take a good look around for food. To help it climb it has five hooked claws on each paw. The bear hugs the trunk with its front paws and hooks its strong, curved claws into the bark. Then it pulls itself up with its front paws and pushes with its back paws. The bear does this so quickly that it looks as if it has leaped up the tree like an agile cat. But unlike cats, bears cannot pull in their claws. A bear's claws are always out and ready for action.

Coming Down

The Black Bear comes down the tree tail first, often dropping the last few metres (yards) to the ground. Although you might be shaken up by such a sudden landing, the Black Bear does not seem to even notice. It just picks itself up and ambles off into the underbrush.

Home Ground

Adult Black Bears keep out of each other's way most of the time. Each bear stakes out a territory that has enough food to keep it alive and healthy. In summer, when there are lots of green plants and berries, a bear's territory may be only three square kilometres (just over one square mile). But in spring, when plants are just beginning to grow and food is scarce, the bear's territory may be ten times as big.

A Black Bear warns other bears away from its territory by posting ''Stay Out'' warnings. To do this it stands on its hind legs beside a tree and claws the bark. Any bears that come along see these claw marks and know they are entering an area that belongs to another bear. They can even tell the size of the bear whose territory they have wandered into. How? The higher the claw marks, the bigger the bear.

Even this handy tree perch won't improve the view. That's because the Black Bear is very nearsighted. But its keen sense of smell and hearing more than make up for its poor eyesight.

Hungry as a Bear

When you think of a bear do you think of a ferocious meat-eating animal? Bears do eat meat, but they also eat plants. That is why they are called omnivores.

The Black Bear is not a picky eater. In fact, it will eat almost anything that is available. Most of its diet is made up of plants, roots, grains and fruit. The bear has very flexible lips and a long tongue which makes berry-picking easy. A bear's favorite fruits include blueberries, strawberries and apples. They also munch on nuts such as acorns, hazelnuts and beechnuts.

This lucky bear cub stops to snack on a special treat—an apple!

In spring, Black Bears that live near the coast dine on migrating salmon. A Black Bear will eat any meat it finds, but it will not normally kill another animal for food unless it is easy prey.

A Black Bear also loves honey, but did you know that it likes to eat bees too? Also high on its list of favorites are ants, grasshoppers, termites and wasps. A bear's thick coat helps protect it from being stung by angry wasps and bees.

Tough Teeth

To chew up all the different kinds of foods it eats, a Black Bear has different kinds of teeth. Sharp pointed meat-cutting teeth for catching prey are in the front of the bear's mouth. Broad flat cheek teeth called molars work like a potato masher to grind up tough plant fibers so the bear can digest them.

Opposite page:

The Black Bear, famous for its sweet tooth, often pokes its nose into tree hollows looking for honey.

Bears Alone and Together

During the summer and fall, a Black Bear is out from dusk to dawn searching for food and eating as much as possible. It needs to put on a good layer of fat in preparation for the long winter ahead when food is hard to find.

Summer is also the only time adult bears are likely to be seen together. That is because it is mating season. Once a bear finds a mate, the two spend a short time together—then they go their separate ways again!

Black Bears are usually loners, except in spring and summer when mom and babies often go down to the woods for a picnic of berries and other tasty treats.

Getting Ready for Winter

When the temperature falls and food becomes scarce, a Black Bear searches for a den in which to have its winter sleep. Finding a warm dry den is especially important for a mother Black Bear who is about to have a family. Long before the first snowfall she begins to inspect caves, hollow logs and overturned stumps for safety and dryness. Once she has chosen a spot, she covers the floor of her winter home with moss, leaves and grasses to make a warm nursery for her family.

Male bears are not nearly as fussy about their dens. They usually wait for the first snowfall before they even start looking for a den. By this time the females have moved into all the best spots. This does not seem to bother the male. If there is no den available, he simply lies down in the shelter of an overturned stump and waits for the snow to fall. As the snow piles up around him, his body warmth melts the snow closest to him, forming a custom-made igloo.

Opposite page:

Bears often gather dead leaves and grass and chewed off sticks as cozy bedding for their dens.

A Long Winter's Sleep

Black Bears in northern areas may nap for up to six months in winter. Bears from warmer regions, where food is available during the winter months, do not need to sleep for so long. Unlike true hibernators, a Black Bear may wake up and even leave its den if the weather is warm enough. When it gets cold again, the bear goes back to its den for another long snooze.

During this long winter's sleep the bear's breathing and heart rate slow down. This means that the bear needs less energy. Instead of having to eat food for energy, it can live on its stored fat.

When a Black Bear wakes up in the spring it is hungry and cranky and its stomach has shrunk because it has not eaten for so long. The first thing it does is look for food and water. Soon the bear's stomach will be full of new plant shoots and tree buds and the bear will be back to its roly-poly self.

Opposite page:

It doesn't matter if the berries are all gone, the bear will still eat the twig.

A Surprise for Mother.

Sows usually give birth to their tiny cubs in January or February, every other year. Mother bears in the north may be fast asleep in their snug dens when their babies are born. Just think of the surprise the mother bear gets when she wakes up and finds she is sharing her den with her new family!

Often there are two cubs, but sometimes there may be as many as five. Newborn Black Bear cubs are about the size of small squirrels. Their eyes are tightly shut, and they do not have any hair or teeth. They spend their first five weeks nursing and snuggling close to their mother's warm, furry body.

These cubs are probably between five and six weeks old. Their eyes are open and their newborn fuzz is being replaced by glossy fur.

Round and Round

When they first start to walk the small cubs have strong front legs and weak, wobbly back legs that they drag behind them. Young cubs cannot crawl in a straight line. Instead they usually go round and round in circles. This means they never get far away from their mother. That is a good thing, because the sow might be fast asleep and unable to keep an eye on them.

A cub gets its first look at the outside world when it is about three months old.

Padded Playground

When they are a week old, the cubs start to grow a fine coat of soft fur. They are able to see their mother for the first time at six weeks, but they are still very wobbly on their feet. Perhaps this is why they tend to spend their time climbing all over their mother, using her warm, furry body as a handy playground.

Bear School

The cubs are only puppy-sized when they leave the den for the first time in mid-April, so their mother keeps a close eye on them at all times. She is gentle and patient but quite strict with her cubs.

By watching their mother throughout their first year, the cubs learn all the skills a bear needs to survive: how to find the right kinds of food, how to look for shelter from bad weather, and what animals—such as cougars, lynxes, Grizzly Bears and adult Black Bears—to avoid.

Opposite page:

If this cub smiled, you might be able to see its milk teeth. Its permanent teeth won't start to grow in until it is nearly three months old.

Overleaf:

Two young cubs follow their mom across a beaver dam.

Weepy Wanderer

If a cub wanders off and gets lost, it cries and whines until its mother tracks it down. She then gently noses the wanderer back to the group. A crying cub is an upset cub; a contented cub purrs rather like a kitten.

When danger approaches the mother hustles the cubs up a tree for safety. But often the playful youngsters will climb trees just for the fun of it. They play tag with each other high in the trees and sunbathe on any convenient branch. In stormy weather, they take shelter in evergreen trees, using the overhanging branches as an umbrella to keep them dry.

Although bears are usually solitary creatures, sometimes two mother bears will travel together with their cubs. The females then share the task of cub-sitting, giving one of the mothers a chance to sleep or eat in peace.

It's amazing how small a branch a big Black Bear can stand on.

On Their Own

The cubs curl up in a den and sleep away the winter with their mother. Their survival lessons start up again in spring and continue until summer when the mother bear starts looking for another mate. At this point the yearlings, now as big as St. Bernard dogs, go on without their mother. However, they often stay with their brother or sister for the rest of the summer and may even share a den that winter.

The following spring, the cubs go their separate ways, putting their newly learned skills to the test. Strong bonds have developed between them, however, and if they meet later in their lives, they will be quite friendly toward each other.

Many trees have scars from the claws of the bears that have climbed them.

Put to the Test

The second year is the most difficult for a young Black Bear. Still small and inexperienced, it must find a territory with enough food to keep it healthy. And it must avoid larger bears, without the help of warning woofs from its mother. If it has learned its lessons well, a wild Black Bear will live to be ten or fifteen years old and have several families of its own.

Special Words

Boar   A male bear.

Cub   Name for the young of various animals, including the Black Bear.

Den   Animal home.

Hibernation   Kind of heavy sleep that some animals take in the winter, during which their breathing and heart rates slow, and their body temperatures go down.

Hibernator   An animal that goes into hibernation for the winter.

Litter   Group of animal brothers and sisters born together.

Mate   To come together to produce young.

Molars   Broad flat cheek teeth that help grind up plant fibers.

Omnivore   An animal that eats plants and meat.

Sow A female bear.

Territory   Area that an animal or group of animals live in and often defend from other animals of the same kind.

INDEX

Cover Photo: Harvey Medland

Photo Credits: Wayne Lankinen (Valan Photos), pages 4, 7, 13, 32, 38; Tim Fitzharris (First Light Associated Photographers), page 10; Norman Lightfoot (Eco-Art Productions), pages 14, 16, 37; T.W. Hall (Parks Canada), page 19; William Lowry (Lowry Photo), pages 20, 24, 29; Bill Ivy, page 23; V. Critch, page 27; J.D. Markou (Valan Photos), page 31; Hälle Flygare (Valan Photos), pages 34-35; Esther Schmidt (Valan Photos), pages 40-41, 42; Barry Ranford, page 45.